MARIE CURIE IN THE LAND OF SCIENCE

Author: Irène Cohen-Janca
Illustrator: Claudia Palmarucci
ISBN: 9781568464008
Price: $20.99

Page count: 56
Hardcover with jacket
Interest level: Age 9 and up
Pub month: August 2025

A Radiant Life

Discoverer of two chemical elements. Winner of two Nobel Prizes. Provider of X-ray examinations for millions of World War I wounded. Despite her fame, the legacy of Polish-born scientist Marie Curie is often linked more to her husband's work than afforded its own due. Author Irène Cohen-Janca gives voice to Marie as illustrator Claudia Palmarucci imbues the images with an almost chemical irradiation in this American adaptation of an Italian publication that was honored with the BolognaRagazzi Award for Nonfiction in 2020.

About the Art

Claudia Palmarucci is an Italian artist and illustrator whose work has appeared in numerous books, including *Marie Curie: In the Land of Science*, which was awarded the 2020 BolognaRagazzi Award for Nonfiction.

CREATIVE EDITIONS

Ali Bryniarski • abryniarski@thecreativecompany.us • (507) 388-6273 ext. 204
Creative Editions is an imprint of The Creative Company • www.thecreativecompany.us

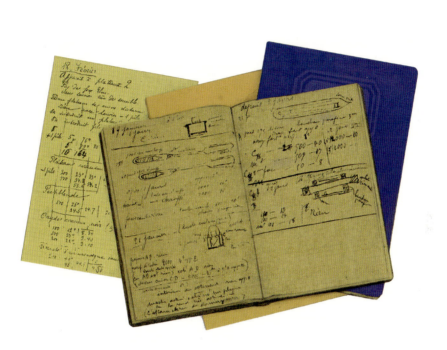

Original title: *Marie Curie au pays de la science* by Irène Cohen-Janca, illustrated by Claudia Palmarucci / First published in Italy under the title *Marie Curie nel paese della scienza* © 2019, orecchio acerbo srl, Roma / English edition published in agreement with Koja Agency Text copyright © 2025 Irène Cohen-Janca / Translation copyright © 2025 Sylvia Notini / Illustrations copyright © 2025 Claudia Palmarucci / Edited by Kate Riggs / Published in 2025 by Creative Editions / P.O. Box 227, Mankato, MN 56002 USA / Creative Editions is an imprint of The Creative Company / www.thecreativecompany.us / All rights reserved. No part of the contents of this book may be reproduced by any means without the written permission of the publisher. / **Library of Congress Cataloging-in-Publication Data**
Names: Cohen-Janca, Irène, 1954- author. | Palmarucci, Claudia, 1985- illustrator. Title: Marie Curie in the Land of Science | by Irène Cohen-Janca; illustrated by Claudia Palmarucci. Other titles: Marie Curie au pays de la science. English Description: English edition. | Mankato, MN : Creative Editions, 2025. "Originally published in 2019 by Orecchio acerbo, Marie Curie au pays de la science, by Irène Cohen-Janca, illustrated by Claudia Palmarucci." | Audience: Ages 9–12 | Audience: Grades 4–6 | Summary: "Narrative biography and detailed illustrations combine to explore important moments in Marie Curie's life and the revolutionary mark she made on science"– Provided by publisher. Identifiers: LCCN 2024043113 (print) | LCCN 2024043114 (ebook) | ISBN 9781568464008 (hardcover) | ISBN 9781640009257 (ebook) | Subjects: LCSH: Curie, Marie, 1867—1934—Juvenile literature. | Women chemists—France—Biography—Juvenile literature. | Chemists—France—Biography—Juvenile literature | Women physicists—France—Biography—Juvenile literature. | Physicists—France—Biography—Juvenile literature. | Women Nobel Prize winners—Biography—Juvenile literature. | Nobel Prize winners—Biography—Juvenile literature. Classification: LCC QD22.C8 C59913 2025 (print) | LCC QD22.C8 (ebook) | DDC 540.92 [B]–dc23/eng/20241119 | LC record available at https://lccn.loc.gov/2024043113 | LC ebook record available at https://lccn.loc.gov/2024043114

First edition 9 8 7 6 5 4 3 2 1 Printed in China

MARIE CURIE
IN THE LAND OF SCIENCE

Irène Cohen-Janca
Illustrated by **Claudia Palmarucci** Translated by **Sylvia Notini**

Creative Editions

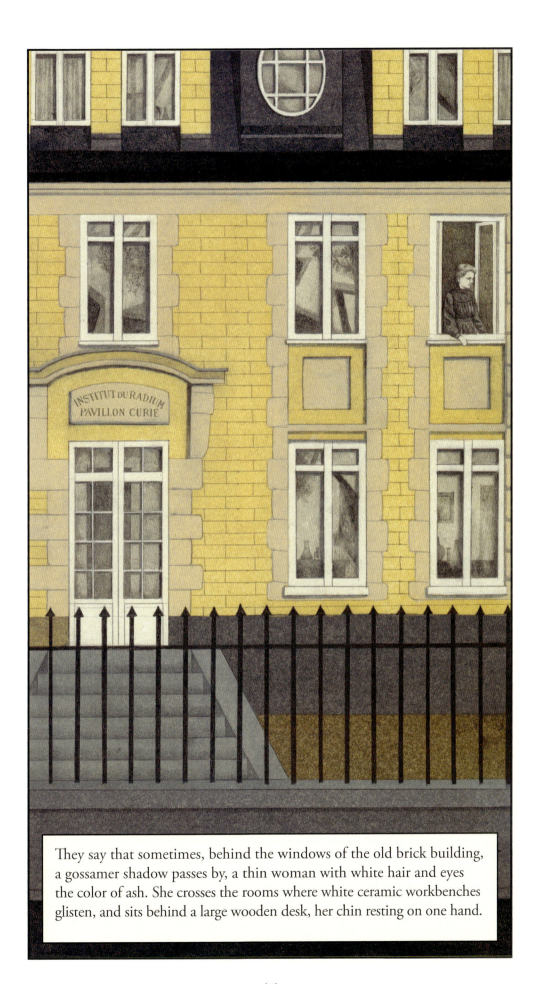

They say that sometimes, behind the windows of the old brick building, a gossamer shadow passes by, a thin woman with white hair and eyes the color of ash. She crosses the rooms where white ceramic workbenches glisten, and sits behind a large wooden desk, her chin resting on one hand.

This old woman used to be young—one of five children in the Skłodowski family. "Mània, Maniusia, Maria, my love, my pet, come here." Madame Skłodowska could not embrace any of her children because she had tuberculosis, a serious, contagious disease. Despite her illness, games and happiness were very much part of the life of the young Skłodowskis: playing, laughing, and most importantly, learning!

Every Saturday, around the samovar, with a look of wonder on their faces, the four daughters—Zosia, Bronia, Hela, Mània—and Józef, the only son, listened to their father read the classics of Polish, English, and French literature to them. What Mània learned from this education would guide her for the rest of her life. There is no greater wealth than learning, culture, knowledge.

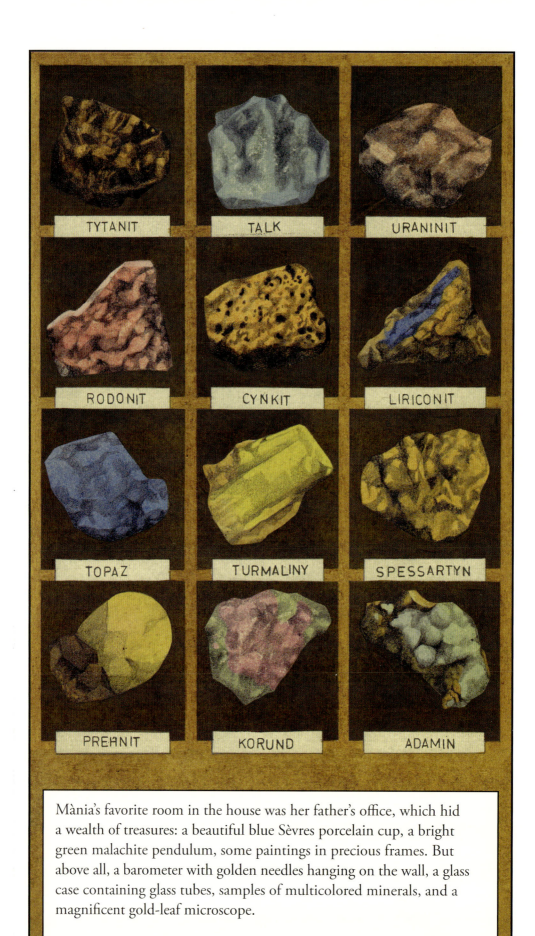

Mània's favorite room in the house was her father's office, which hid a wealth of treasures: a beautiful blue Sèvres porcelain cup, a bright green malachite pendulum, some paintings in precious frames. But above all, a barometer with golden needles hanging on the wall, a glass case containing glass tubes, samples of multicolored minerals, and a magnificent gold-leaf microscope.

Mània found all these objects enchanting. "They are instruments used for physics," her father told her. With her lovely gray eyes Mània never tired of contemplating them: "physics instruments, physics instruments …"

In January 1876, typhoid took her sister, Zosia.

Then 10-year-old Mània donned black mourning clothes when her beloved mother died in May 1878. She felt terribly alone. Bronia, her older sister, took over running the household.

Mània finished secondary school and graduated with the highest possible award, a gold medal. Her thirst for knowledge was insatiable, but in Poland girls did not have access to higher education. Furthermore, Poland was living under Russian rule. At school, at the university, it was forbidden to even speak Polish.

A group of professors decided to create a secret university. During the night, in the freezing apartments of Warsaw, courses in history, literature, math, and natural sciences were taught. For two years, Mània and Bronia attended these classes. Mània also taught women who were poor, she gave readings in the workshops, and she created a small library.

The two sisters agreed that Bronia would go to Paris, enroll in the university, and Mània would stay and work to support them.

Once Bronia became a doctor, she would in turn pay for Mània's studies.

Mània accepted a position as a governess for a family of wealthy industrialists in a far-away province. On the cold and foggy morning of January 1, 1886, Mània left Warsaw for field after field of beets and clayey soil for as far as the eye could see. Soon, Mània forged connections with the families who worked that land, teaching their children to read and write.

She had lots of science books shipped to her, and at night she continued to study on her own. She was devoured by the same thirst for knowledge as ever. Sometimes, however, the desperation, discouragement, and bitterness would get the better of her. In December 1886 she wrote these words to her cousin: *"My dreams have gone up in smoke, I have buried them, shut them off, hidden and forgotten them—because, as you well know, walls are always stronger than the heads that try to tear them down."*

Finally, in 1889, Mània went back to Warsaw to live and work. Five long, sad years had gone by, until one day in March 1890, when Bronia, who in the meantime had become a doctor and gotten married, wrote to Mània: *"Next year you will come to Paris and live with us."* At last, it was Mània's turn. She was ready to tear down all the walls that were keeping her apart from her dreams.

In November 1891, the transcontinental train left 24-year-old Mània standing on the smoke-filled platforms of the Gare du Nord. No sooner had she put her things away and settled into Bronia's home than she raced to the Palace of Wisdom, the Temple of Knowledge: the Sorbonne. She enrolled under the name Marie Skłodowska, ready to get a degree in science.

Marie had to come to terms with her own lack of knowledge in physics and math, and even in French. She worked without ceasing, and she slept and ate very little. In the evening, she studied in the great library of Sainte-Geneviève until ten, and after that in her tiny room until three in the morning, with the light of an oil lamp burning next to a freezing cold heater.

One day, Marie was so worn out, she fainted. Bronia's husband, also a doctor, went to see her.
"What did you eat today?" he asked.
"I'm not sure ... some cherries and radishes, perhaps."
"What about yesterday?"
"A bunch of radishes."
"Well, come on then, come with me. A couple of steaks and some proper rest will do the trick!"

In July 1893, she raced to the Sorbonne to find out the results of her physics degree exam. As the president of the exam board was about to speak, a hush came over the great amphitheater: "First in her class, Mademoiselle Marie Skłodowska." Later, in 1894, she would be second in her class for a degree in mathematics.

Marie had but one passion, and that was science—until a spring day in 1894, when she met Pierre Curie. He was already an important scientist who had made some major discoveries, a man who was driven by the same passion and the same ideals as Marie.

Pierre cared nothing for money or honors; he loathed the competitive spirit. Pierre would spend hours discussing physics problems with Marie. Instead of flowers and chocolate candy, he gave her science textbooks. She told him about her childhood dreams, about her long walks in the woods.

That summer, when she went to Poland to visit her father and stayed there to teach, Pierre wrote to her: *"I would be greatly saddened if you were not to come back this year."* But Marie did return, and on July 26, 1895, she and Pierre were married in Sceaux.

That year, in Germany, Professor Wilhelm Röntgen had discovered some strange rays that could cross solid matter such as wood, aluminum, and human flesh. The rays were called X-rays because X symbolizes the unknown in math.

Soon afterwards, French physicist Henri Becquerel discovered some other invisible rays. But this time, they came from a mineral called uranium.

Marie was curious—where did the energy emitted by uranium come from? She began by analyzing the composition of a uranium-rich rock known as pitchblende.

Discovering and isolating the elements besides uranium that were contained in pitchblende was difficult. The work conditions were miserable. Tons of minerals needed to be treated, which were delivered by carriage from Bohemia to the laboratory courtyard.

On July 18, 1898, Pierre and Marie discovered a new metal, which they called polonium, in memory of Poland. But hiding inside those pitch-black rocks was another substance: radium.

After processing eight tons of pitchblende, the Curies finally managed to extract a gram of radium in 1904. They were amazed at the marvelous substance lying in tiny Petri dishes and its beautiful shade of blue glowing in the night.

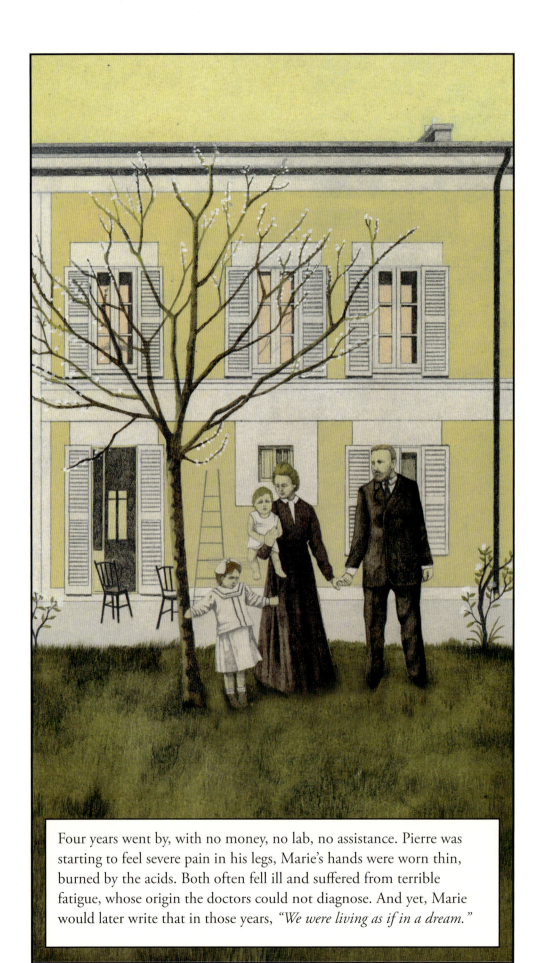

Four years went by, with no money, no lab, no assistance. Pierre was starting to feel severe pain in his legs, Marie's hands were worn thin, burned by the acids. Both often fell ill and suffered from terrible fatigue, whose origin the doctors could not diagnose. And yet, Marie would later write that in those years, *"We were living as if in a dream."*

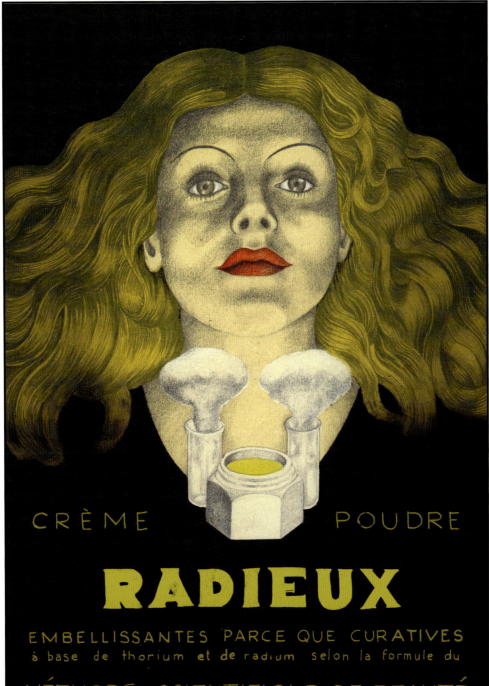

It was an absolute revolution! Their discovery was about to transform physics completely. A new source of energy was born, and it came directly from matter. Radium could replace wood, charcoal. Some doctors began using radium to treat tumors. But you had to know how to extract the radium, and only the Curies knew how to do that.

When questions started coming in from around the world, Pierre asked Marie: "Can we consider ourselves the owners, the 'inventors' of radium ... and get the world royalties for its production?" They could earn a fortune—all they had to do was take out a patent. But Marie wouldn't hear of it. They chose to reveal to the world's scientists the results of their research.

On December 10, 1903, Marie and Pierre, along with Henri Becquerel, received the Nobel Prize, the highest scientific honor of all, for their research on radioactivity. Marie was the first woman ever to be awarded a Nobel Prize.

Their fame was instant, and reporters and photographers from around the world followed their every move. Even Didì, the family cat, became famous. The United States offered the Curies huge amounts of money to give talks.

They missed the days when they were both unknown. *"We would like to burrow a tunnel underground and find some peace,"* Marie wrote to her brother. Pierre was finally named professor of physics at the Sorbonne, but the "real" lab that he had been dreaming of for years hadn't been built yet.

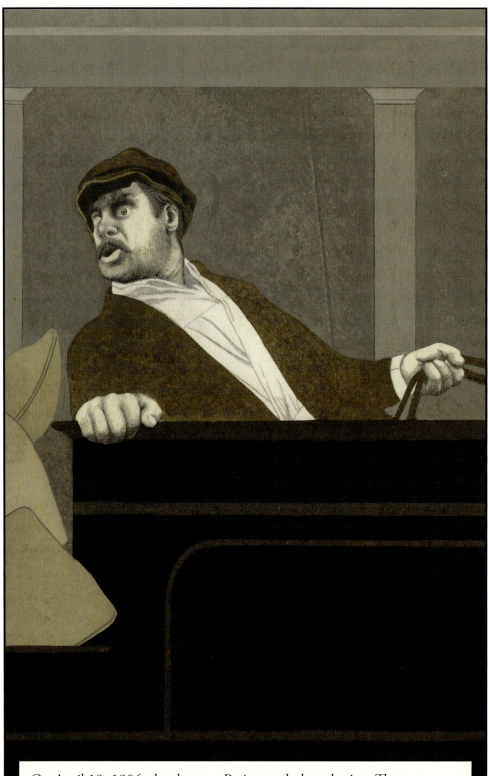

On April 19, 1906, the sky over Paris was dark and rainy. The narrow, crowded streets were full of shouting coachmen, screeching trams, and rumbling automobiles. Suddenly, a heavily laden wagon drawn by two horses appeared on Rue Dauphine. Pierre Curie was walking behind a carriage holding a big black umbrella over his head, and he failed to see it. He was killed instantly, crushed by the hooves of the heavy horses.

Marie was now alone with two young daughters, Irène and Eve, who were just nine and two. She was asked to take over Pierre's teaching position at the Sorbonne.

After much deliberation, Marie took her husband's place as Professor of General Physics in the Faculty of Sciences. On November 5, 1906, before a packed amphitheater, Marie gave her first lecture. After being the first woman ever to receive a Nobel Prize, she became the first woman to hold a university chair in France.

·EXCELSIOR·
Journal Illustré Quotidien

L'Académie des Sciences examine aujourd'hui la candidature de Mme Curie

Conseil de Physique Solvay 1911

Marie Curie et Albert Einstein

M.me Curie

Although Marie routinely taught her lessons, she continued to do research. And she shone brightly within the international scientific community, alongside luminaries such as Einstein, Rutherford, and Planck.

Then she received the most extraordinary news of all: Marie had been awarded the Nobel Prize for Chemistry, for her discovery of radium and polonium. For the first time ever, a winner was crowned for a second time.

At last, the Radium Institute could now be built. "*Research laboratories are the sacred places of the future,*" wrote Marie when the project for a real laboratory finally saw the light. However, once the two-year project was complete, it was August 1914, and war was soon declared.

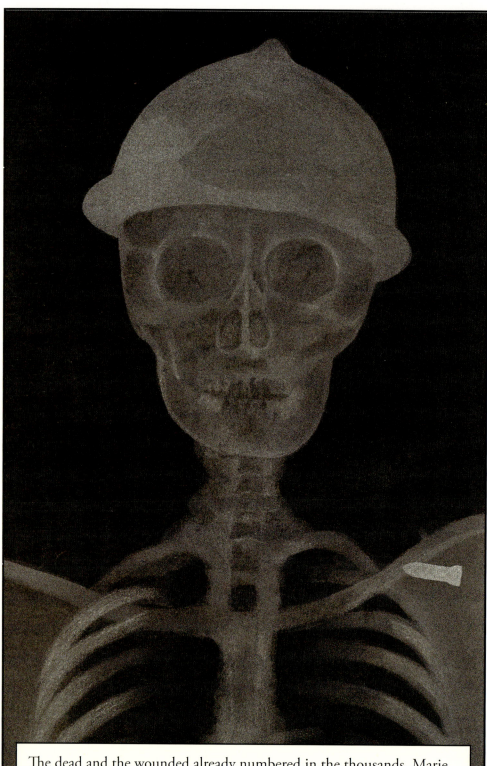

The dead and the wounded already numbered in the thousands. Marie recalled Röntgen's famous X-rays that made it possible to explore the human body, to photograph the bones and the organs. X-rays could help surgeons identify a bullet from a rifle, shrapnel in the body of the wounded, and help them do their job with great precision.

But there were very few Röntgen machines, just two or three in the Paris hospitals. And the army had only one radiological ambulance. Armed with the prestige of her name, Marie started her campaigning at the Ministries. She visited all the richest families—several princesses lent her their cars, beautiful limousines and vans to which she had the necessary equipment added. She even went to see the automobile manufacturers in Paris and the suburbs.

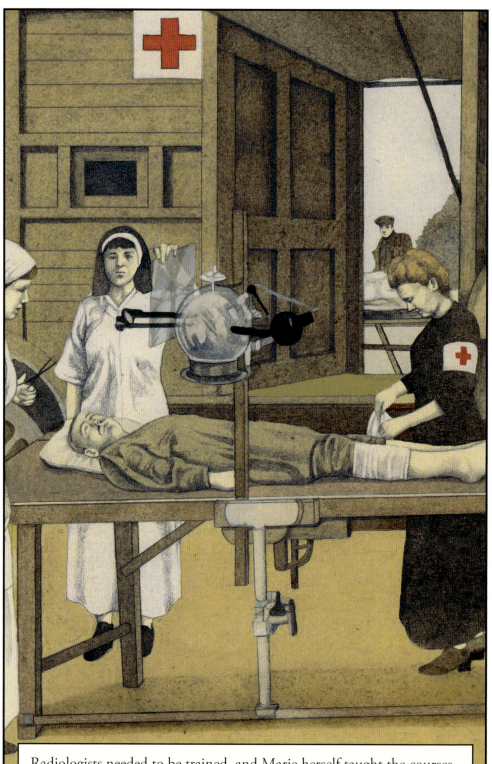

Radiologists needed to be trained, and Marie herself taught the courses with the help of one of her students, Marthe Klein, and her daughter Irène. She had 200 X-ray machines installed in the military hospitals and equipped 20 automobiles that plowed the battlefields. As a tribute to Marie's bravery and determination, the ambulances were nicknamed "Petites Curies."

Marie got a driver's license so that she could drive a Petite Curie herself. This famous woman could be seen driving back and forth across the battlefields, wearing a threadbare black alpaca coat, a Red Cross band around her arm, a small faded and floppy round hat perched on her head, and carrying a shabby yellow leather bag. More than a million wounded received X-ray examinations, thanks to the Petites Curies and the field hospitals.

When peace finally returned, Marie went back to her lab and to the experiments she had begun before the war. One morning in May 1920, an American journalist and great admirer of Marie's, Mrs. Meloney, went to see her. She asked Marie what she wished for most in the world. Marie replied, "I would need a gram of radium to continue with my research." A single gram was worth one hundred thousand dollars.

Mrs. Meloney launched a huge campaign and collected the amount of money that was needed. One year later, United States president Warren Harding presented Marie with a box lined with lead as he placed a cloth ribbon with a tiny golden key around her neck. Inside the box was the precious gram of radium.

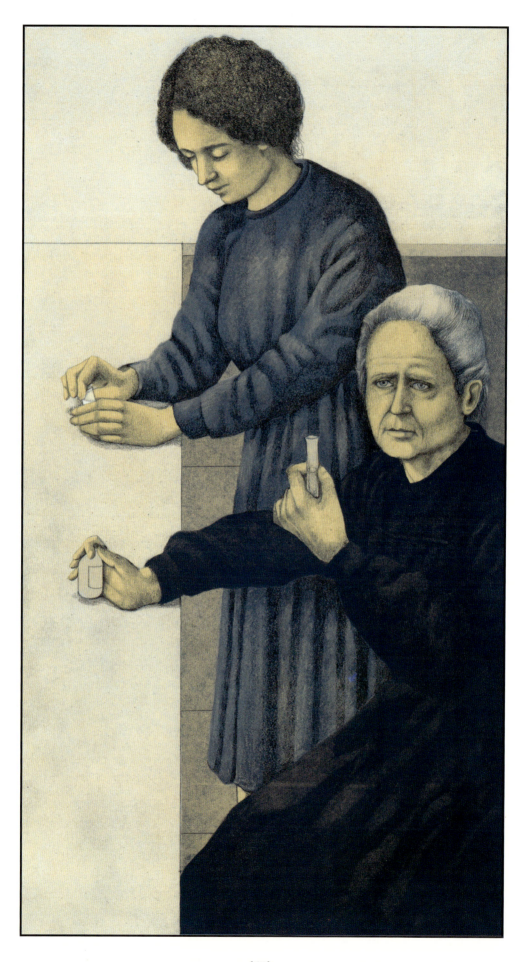

Then Marie got sick. Her beautiful gray eyes became veiled. She underwent numerous operations to retrieve her eyesight. Although she became weaker by the day, she never stopped researching, teaching, and running the Radium Institute.

One sunlit afternoon in May 1934, Marie took a walk in the garden of the Institute where she admired the spring colors.

Marie would never return to her lab, nor would she ever again stroll through her garden. The doctors had just begun diagnosing the illness that was consuming her. Her illness was caused by the radium and its rays, to which Marie Curie had been exposing herself without any protection for thirty-five years. She died on July 3, 1934.

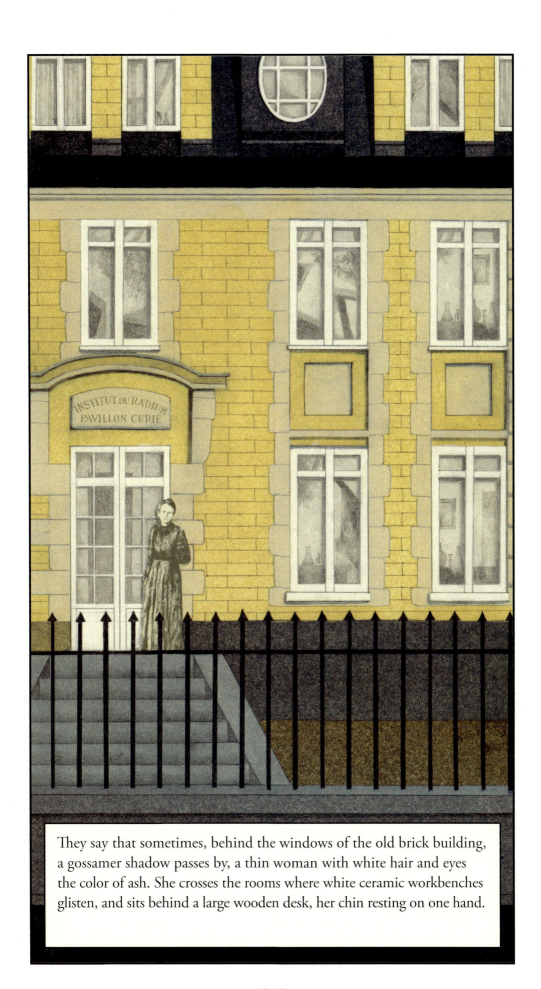

They say that sometimes, behind the windows of the old brick building, a gossamer shadow passes by, a thin woman with white hair and eyes the color of ash. She crosses the rooms where white ceramic workbenches glisten, and sits behind a large wooden desk, her chin resting on one hand.

Illustration Notes

Page 1: An illustration of Marie and Pierre Curie's manuscripts, currently preserved with a high level of security because they are still radioactive.

Page 9: The leaf electroscope is used to determine whether a body is electrically charged. When a charged object is brought near the electroscope terminal, the electric field from the object induces a charge in the conductive electroscope, and the leaves repel each other and thus open. If, instead, the object is not charged, gravity aligns the two leaves, which hang down vertically. The phenomenon is based on one of the essential properties of electrostatic induction: objects with the same electric charge repel each other.

Page 12: The image, which is chronologically unrelated to the narrative, shows Marie as a young girl. Marie was the youngest and smallest of her peers, but she was also the one who spoke the best Russian. This explains why she was often tested orally about Russian history or asked to recite a poem during the much-feared visits of the Russian inspectors. The episode is recalled in detail in Eve Marie's book about her mother and bears witness to Marie's deep feelings of restlessness during her school years.

Page 33: During the years of its discovery, radium was publicized as being a cure-all. Radium was added to toothpaste and creams, it was used to treat cancer, lupus, and all sorts of other problems. Unfortunately, the mutagenic effects caused by continuous exposure to radiation were still unknown at the time, although Pierre had already intuited that this element was potentially and dangerously toxic. He spoke about it in his Nobel Prize acceptance speech. The discovery of radium was soon exploited in the advertising strategies of many industries. The Tho-Radia cosmetics brand, for instance, launched a cream with a "thorium and radium base," described as patented by one Dr. Alfred Curie, who shared Pierre's last name but was unknown to the scientists. My illustration is a new version of that poster. I added the two test tubes of ice water as it evaporates, thus creating a sort of atomic mushroom. In those years, Pierre published an article that unveiled a rather surprising discovery: a single gram of radium could make one gram of ice water reach boiling temperature in one hour. A historian of science identified this discovery as "the first appearance, in human affairs, of atomic energy in the familiar form of heat" (Quinn, p. 225).

Page 35: In 1903, the members of the Academy of Sciences nominated Pierre Curie for the Nobel Prize, completely overlooking Marie's role in the discovery of radioactivity. However, it was impossible to ignore her major contribution to the work and to the results. Pierre replied to the letter he received announcing his candidacy as follows: "If it is true that one is seriously thinking about me (for the Prize), I very much wish to be considered together with Madame Curie with respect to our research on radioactive bodies." During the ceremony, Pierre alone taught the lesson, although he mentioned Marie several times. This is why I chose to portray her seated.

Page 40: Illustration inspired by Winslow Homer's *Blackboard* (1877).

Page 50: Next to Marie is Irène Joliot-Curie. The daughter of Pierre and Marie and the sister of Eve, Irène continued her parents' studies, and in 1935, she and her husband Frédéric Joliot won the Nobel Prize for Chemistry.

These are just a few of my observations as concerns the illustrations I made for this book. It would be impossible to describe the huge amount of material I examined over the months of work, without which it would have been rather difficult to even approach this scientist's life.

I especially wish to mention the indispensable and highly accurate biography by Susan Quinn, *Marie Curie: A Life* (Da Capo, 1996). I also found a great deal of information in the biography that Eve Curie wrote just three years after her mother passed away, *Madame Curie: A Biography* (Da Capo, 2001), as well as in Marie Curie's own autobiography, an Italian version of which was published by Castelvecchi in 2019. For the historical, cultural, and scientific material I needed for the illustrations, I found there was a wealth of material online and, in particular, a vast amount of data made available for consultation by the Musée Curie website. Lastly, the many past and recent films and documentaries dedicated to Marie Curie helped me to recreate the places and the settings of this great scientist's life.

Claudia Palmarucci